Broken. Wounded. Healed.

A Story of God's Redemption

By Stacie Taylor

Tina,
May God bless you
in all you do.

☺ - Stacie
Taylor

Edited and formatted by Katie Erickson.

ISBN-13: 978-1546500599
ISBN-10: 1546500596

I dedicate this book to all those who helped me and my family in a time of need. Thank you for allowing God to use you to bless me and my family. You will forever hold a special place in my heart. I pray that I will be able to make a difference in someone's life the way you have mine. Thank you for being Jesus to me.

Foreword

For seven years, I was in a marriage that was filled with deception, betrayal, hurt, abuse, and lies. Oh, the joy I felt the day God delivered me and my two small babies from this man! I felt the hand of God wrap around us in a way that flamed my faith into total surrender. I am about to tell you how God intervened when I gave Him complete control of my life. I am here today because of *Him*. I am who I am today because of *Him*. I am excited about tomorrow because of *Him*. I am nothing without *Him*.

I was once blinded by things of this world, but Jesus opened my eyes to the life He willingly sacrificed for me to have. I rely on Him alone to carry me through my day. He gives me the confidence and strength I need to do what He has called me to do.

Peace. I love the sound of this word but I love the feeling of it more. Knowing that you are where God wants you to be brings the kind of peace that nothing in this world can. I hope you know that peace today.

I often hear people say, "Why would a loving God allow terrible things to happen? Why doesn't God protect us from bad things?" Looking back over my trials, I often wondered why God allowed me to experience what I did. I stand here today to tell you that it has made me who I am today, a woman after God's heart.

I am here to tell my story of wounds, my brokenness, and God's healing in my life. Unlocking the memories is painful, but my story will reveal the complete power of our Almighty God.

Table of Contents

Chapter 1

"Just then, a woman who had suffered from bleeding for 12 years approached from behind and touched the tassel on His robe, for she said to herself, 'If I can just touch His robe, I'll be made well!'
But Jesus turned and saw her. 'Have courage, daughter,' He said. 'Your faith has made you well.' And the woman was made well from that moment." (Matthew 9:20-22, HCSB)

Wow! What joy this woman must have experienced that day! I had the same experience the day I surrendered my pain, my worries, and my life to God. I didn't have to physically touch His robe; through my faith I was made well. I am confident of this because my Jesus tells me every day. He uses circumstances, His word and the joy I feel in my heart to confirm that He has healed my soul. Through faith I have been made well.

For seven years, I was married to an addict. I knew that I should not have married this man. God told me not to marry this man. But, I chose my path instead of His. The moment I chose my path instead of God's, I stopped hearing His voice. I stopped feeling His presence.

I was tired of waiting, so I turned my back on God. Instead of waiting for Him to show me the one He had chosen for me, I chose for myself. Boy, was I ever wrong. I would soon find out what God was trying to protect me from.

Seven years of abuse was waiting for me just around the corner. Seven years of hurt, betrayal, lies, disappointments, and fear, all from my selfish desire.

He was what I thought to be a "social drinker" when we were dating. After we married, the drinking became worse. I watched him change shortly after we were married to someone I no longer recognized. I started blaming myself for his actions. I felt as if I was not good enough for him. I noticed how he seemed unhappy with the choice he made – his choice of me.

Unworthy. Unloved. Unwanted. These feelings consumed me as the enemy gripped me with hands of loneliness as he poured these lies into my heart: lies that I was unwanted from the time I was born; lies that no one would ever love me because something was wrong with me. Because I felt that something was wrong with me, I felt that I was unworthy of anyone loving me. Instead of refusing to believe these lies, I allowed myself to fall into this bondage and found myself in a deep pit of despair. I wanted so badly to be loved.

I would find calls he made to his past girlfriends on our phone bill. He would tell me that a "friend" was going through a difficult time and he needed to go be with them and stay gone overnight, not realizing he was cheating on me. I found out I was pregnant a year after we were married.

After my son was born, I thought things would improve, but they didn't. When my son was six months old, I found out I was pregnant with my daughter. I became a stay at home mom after my son was born. When my husband came home from work, he would lock himself in the bedroom, watch TV, and drink. Some days I would come home to find him passed out in the floor drunk. I would pick him up and place him in the shower, clothes and all, and turn on the cold water. He would jump out of the shower swinging his arms at me. At times, I would be afraid to come home in fear I would find him dead. Several times he would have to go to the ER to have his stomach pumped after I would find him passed out with bottles of narcotics lying beside him, not knowing home many pills he swallowed.

The next day I would hear the same lines over and over: "I'm sorry. I promise to never drink again." Each time I heard this I knew it was a lie. The control started after we were married. He made me think he was protecting me and I fell for it. When the drinking became worse, so did the control.

I was not allowed to have friends. When my friends would call, he would ask them what they wanted and why they were calling. Eventually, the calls stopped. I became more isolated and alone. The verbal abuse started, and then the physical abuse. I remember once I accidentally stepped on his toe and he punched me in the stomach.

He made me choose between him and my family. My family disliked him and he knew it.

He degraded me in front of others as well. After I became a stay at home mom, we went to the bank so he could add me to the account. He started flirting with the woman at the counter, then looked at me and said, "Are you sure I can trust you with my money?" He thought he was being funny as he looked at the lady and gave her a wink. The lady gave me a look of pity and I felt so small.

He would get drunk and try to pick up my kids to play with them. I would pry them from his arms, trying not to anger him, but out of fear of him hurting them. He would try to leave drunk and stumble to his truck and pass out in the driveway. It was cold outside and I struggled with the thought of locking the door and leaving him outside until he woke the next morning, or maybe he would freeze to death and I would be free from him. My conscience would tell me no, so I would go drag him back in the house, hoping my neighbors would not notice.

Each day, I continued to call out to God. Silence. After the long silence, I started to believe the lies of the enemy. I had made a decision to turn from God, so this was what I deserved. But deep down I still held on to hope. I continued to pray and call out to Him.

Even though I felt I had ruined my life, I had to believe God was going to hear my prayers as I prayed daily over my children. I took them to church, I read them all the Bible stories, and I taught them how to pray. Each day I continued to press my way through my madness just so I could get close enough to reach out and touch the garment of Jesus, just like the lady in the story. I knew that if I could just get close enough to touch the hem of His garment, I would be made whole again.

One day I was at the sink washing dishes while listening to the radio. After the song ended, I heard the radio host say, "Do you feel alone? Do you feel unappreciated? Do you feel like you give your all and no one sees you? Well, I just want to encourage you to keep doing what you are doing because God sees you."

I was washing dishes for the third time that day (we didn't have a dishwasher) as my kids were playing together on the floor nearby. I was so tired, so lonely and so desperate. I asked God, "Do you see me?"

Suddenly, I felt this little hand on my leg, I looked down and it was my son. He was about fourteen months old at the time, and he was looking up at me with the sweetest smile on his face. His eyes were filled with a peace that I had never seen before. We became frozen in this moment as I stared into his eyes as he continued to smile up at me. I felt the Holy Spirit fill my body with a peace that can only come from God Himself. I then heard God say, "I see you."

As the peace of God's presence flowed through me, I quickly realized that I was looking into the face of God! He was looking up at me through the face of my child. After what seemed like a few minutes, my son snapped out of his trance and went back to being his crazy little self.

I wish I could explain the feeling of peace that flowed through me as I stood in the presence of God Almighty that day. Finally, I felt the presence of my Almighty Heavenly Father that I had longed to hear from for so long! It was at that moment as I pressed my way through my madness, just to get close enough to reach out and touch the garment of Jesus, that He reached down and touched me. He made me whole again. I praised Him in that moment and asked for forgiveness.

I explained how ashamed I was for the decisions I had made. I told Him that I was never again choosing my way. From now on, it was going to be His way. God placed a verse in my heart that day: "Be still and know that I am God" (Psalm 46:10a, NKJV).

That is exactly what I did. I watched Him work out every single detail of my life after that day. Every. Single. Detail. I cannot wait to tell you all about the amazing things He did for me.

"We know that all things work together for the good of those who love God: those who are called according to His purpose." (Romans 8:28, HCSB)

I love that we can cry out to Him in faith, reach out to grab His robe, and know that He will heal us. This is the kind of faith that Jesus wants us to have. I was once blinded by things of this world, but Jesus opened my eyes to the love He so freely gives, an unconditional love. I rely on Him alone to carry me through my day. He gives me the confidence and strength I need to do what He has planned for me. This strength and confidence is how I know I am where God wants me to be.

Years later, as I prepared to tell this story to a group of ladies from my church, these questions came to me: Why did God wait so long to reveal Himself to me? Why was He silent for so long? Why did He allow me to suffer for all those years? I asked God and this was His answer: "I was preparing a glorious moment where I would reveal Myself to you in such an amazing and inspiring way to show you my power, grace and mercy. I was writing your story to reveal My glory."

What are you struggling with today? Pain? Despair? I want to challenge you to reach out and touch the hem of His garment and you too will be made well.

"Consider it a great joy, my brothers, whenever you experience various trials, knowing that the testing of your faith produces endurance. But endurance must do its complete work, so that you may be mature and complete, lacking nothing." (James 1:2-4, HCSB)

Chapter 2

"Come to Me all of you who are weary and burdened, and I will give you rest." (Matthew 11:28, HCSB)

A few years had passed since God revealed Himself to me and things were starting to go downhill fast. My kids and I were not safe. We had moved six times in six years. I finally realized that my husband was stealing narcotics from the hospital he worked at and when he was close to getting caught, he would get another job. He would lie to me and tell me that the job was too stressful and he needed a change. Our last move was from North Carolina to Arizona, 2100 miles away from my family. I felt alone, scared, and tired. I poured my heart out to God: "God, you know this man's heart. Please protect us from him. I trust you and I will not move until you tell me." He eventually lost his nursing license after finally being caught stealing narcotics. He then became a personal trainer at a local gym and I had to go find a job. His mom lived in Arizona and helped with the kids while I worked as a receptionist at an assisted living facility nearby. He was always high on narcotics or drunk. He was a "functioning alcoholic." I forgot what it was like to see him sober. It became so bad that my neighbors, whom I barely knew, were offering their support for me and my kids.

Shortly after that prayer, a thought came to me. I quickly realized that God was speaking to me and I had to act fast. God told me I needed to take our birth certificates, social security cards, and any other papers that were of importance, put them in a folder and hide them in a safe place, a place my husband would never find. God was very specific that day and I knew I was being prepared for something.

I will always remember the fear that I had. It was a fear that I hope to never experience again. The papers I needed to gather were kept in the closet locked up in a box. The key to that box was on his set of car keys. He kept these keys with him at all times. He would lay them on the bedside table close to where he slept at night. After he passed out from a long day of drinking mixed with narcotics, I had to sneak in the bedroom, get down on my hands and knees and crawl on my stomach around the bed to the nightstand.

My whole body was shaking as I tried to not make a sound. My eyes gazed under the bed and saw several empty wine and liquor bottles. The rancid smell of sweat and alcohol filled the room. I listened intently to his long, deep breaths that told me that he was still sleeping. I reached up to grab the keys and tried hard to keep them from rattling in my hands. I felt a sense of excitement and fear as I crawled my way back around the bed and finally into the closet. As I listened to his long, deep breaths, I closed the closet door behind me. Carefully, I opened the lock box and pulled out all the important documents. I knew it was not over; I still had to put the keys back. Back on my stomach I went and slowly made my way back to the dresser. Once the keys were placed back in their spot, I crawled to the door. That was the longest forty-five minutes of my life. I placed the papers in a folder and hid them in the kids' closet. Then I waited. One month later, I would find out what God was preparing me for.

I was getting ready for work one morning and could not find my keys. I walked into the kitchen and my purse was emptied out on the table and my bank card and keys were missing. I woke him up to ask where my keys were. I was already late for work. I will never forget the smell that filled the room. It was a familiar smell and it made me sick to my stomach. As he climbed out of bed with a disheveled look, he told me he was going to drive me to work and that I was not allowed to drive myself anywhere anymore without his permission. He reached under the mattress and pulled out my car keys. My heart started racing and I knew it was time. I told him I was leaving, that I was no longer living under his control. We were living in Arizona at this time and I knew that I needed to call my family back in North Carolina. I looked around for the phone after noticing it was not on the receiver. I looked around and found it hidden under the bed. As I reached for it, I felt his arm close around my neck, and all of a sudden I was being lifted off the floor. I couldn't talk, breathe, or move. He was choking me and the whole time I kept saying in my head, "He's choking me, he's really choking me!" Then, I passed out.

The first thing I remembered was the sound of my kids crying as I felt myself floating through a dark tunnel heading towards a light. When I regained consciousness, I noticed I could not move my arms. I quickly realized he was holding me down on the bed. I fought my way loose from his grip and grabbed my kids who were standing at the end of the bed crying. I was then told to tell my kids goodbye because my life was about to end. He went to the closet and pulled out the gun. He then reached for the phone and called his mom to come pick up the kids. While he was on the phone, he stared at me with threatening eyes, daring me to make a move. I just sat on the bed holding my two babies trying to keep them calm as I also tried to calm myself. I will always remember his next words: "If you make a move, I will choke you again."

His mom rang the doorbell and he told me to stay put. He went to the door and I ran into the living room to tell his mom what had happened. She looked at me in disbelief. She didn't believe me!

She then suggested that she take the kids and her son with her to her house as if I was the bad person. I would not let her take my kids. The next few hours would seem like days. After I denied her request and explained to her she was not taking my kids I took the kids to their room and played with them to try to keep things "normal," like everything was ok. He would stand in the doorway and watch my every move with the gun by his side. I tried to ignore him as the kids and I played with the train set on the floor. After a few minutes, he walked back out into the living room with his mom.

I then heard her scream, "Get out! Get the kids and get out!" I grabbed the kids by their hands and we ran for the front door. As we came around the corner, my heart sank. The couch had been moved in front of the door so we could not leave. I turned and ran back into the kids' room and closed the door and locked it. On my way back to the room, I glanced over and saw his mom struggling to pull a gun away from his head. After I shut the door I covered my kids' ears with my hands as I waited for the sound of the gun to go off. A few minutes went by and it was silent, then he opened the door and walked in, the gun still in his hand. He stood in the doorway and silently watched my every move. If I tried to walk out of the bedroom he would run up to me and block my way so I could not leave the room. I continued to play with the kids to try to keep things "normal" in their eyes. I knew that I had to do what I could to protect them.

I never showed up to work that morning. I knew that if I could get him to let me make a phone call, I could alert someone. He handed me the phone after I explained how I would lose my job if I didn't call in. As he handed me the phone, I told him I was too nervous and he needed to call in for me. A month earlier, I had told a few girls that I work with about his alcohol abuse and they knew how controlling he was. If they heard him call in for me, I knew that they would be concerned. It worked. He called the office, told them we had a family emergency and I would not be coming to work that day.

Thirty minutes passed while he let me fix the kids' breakfast as I continued to keep them distracted.

Suddenly, there was a knock at the door. Two girls I worked with had come to check on me. He opened the door and hid the gun behind his back. I stood in the background crying silently, unable to say a word. They saw me as I stood there frozen, afraid to speak or move. He told them that everything was fine and closed the door. After they left, he became worried that they would call the cops.

I knew this was it; this was my chance to get him out of the apartment. I was able to talk him into leaving with his mom. She had agreed to take him to the hospital for help. I just wanted him to leave. Miraculously, he agreed to leave. As he walked out the door with his mom, he took two things with him, his gun and the lock box. This was the same lock box that had once contained our important documents.

I will always remember that feeling of fear after he left. I was numb and paralyzed. I grabbed my kids and ran outside. I knocked on my neighbor's door and no one answered. I went from door to door; no answer. I felt like I was the only person in the world. I couldn't think, I didn't know what to do. The world was silent. I ran back inside and searched for a phone. I couldn't find the one that was hidden under the bed and figured that he must have taken that with him. After digging through the closet, I finally found the other cordless phone that he had hidden. I think I dialed my sister's number five times before I got it right. She answered and I was barely able to get my words out because of how hard I was crying. I quickly told her what happened and she immediately started working on getting plane tickets for us to fly back to North Carolina. Shortly after we hung up, the cops arrived. The girls I worked with had called them just as I had hoped they would.

My sweet little boy looked up at the cop and said, "My daddy had a gun and put it to his head like this." He put his tiny fingers, shaped like a gun, up to his forehead to show the cop. My heart broke as I witnessed what this sweet, innocent little boy will forever remember about this day. After filling out a police report and answering many questions, I was asked if I wanted to press charges. I knew that we would soon be over a thousand miles away from this man, so in that moment I said no. His aunt and uncle lived in the area and they came over ready to help. My sister had called them. The kids and I packed what we could fit into three suitcases and we headed to their house to wait for our flight back home. They cared for us and helped us in every way they could.

We left with the clothes on our back, what I could fit in our suitcase and $170 from a bonus check I received at my job the week before. The next day I found out that he had taken my name off our bank account. With no access to money, I took the check and cashed it knowing that was all the money I had to care for me and my kids. I trusted God to provide for us; after all, He had brought us this far. I dropped by my job to say my goodbyes and thanked the girls that saved our lives. The kids and I caught a taxi to the airport and boarded the plane.

The five-hour flight was a scary but exciting time for me. I was free. I was alive. I was turning my whole and complete self to my heavenly Father. Never again will I choose my path in life. From now on, I choose God. He was giving me a second chance at life and I was so grateful yet felt so undeserving.

The court system later read my police report. In the state of Arizona, if a child is involved in a domestic violence case, the case is taken over by the state. A warrant was put out for my husband's arrest and he was found shortly after and arrested. He pleaded guilty and was placed on probation. I was awarded a three-year restraining order.

A few months later, God brought me to Psalm 18. I knew God was saying, "Look what I did for you! I will never leave nor forsake you my child." As I read through this passage, I became overwhelmed with tears of joy as I realized that God had orchestrated every event of that day!

Psalm 18 (HCSB) says:

I love You, Lord, my strength. The Lord is my rock, my fortress, and my deliverer, my God, my mountain where I seek refuge, my shield and the horn of my salvation, my stronghold. I called to the Lord, who is worthy of praise, and I was saved from my enemies. The ropes of death were wrapped around me; the torrents of destruction terrified me. The ropes of Sheol entangled me; the snares of death confronted me. I called to the Lord in my distress, and I cried to my God for help. From His temple He heard my voice, and my cry to Him reached His ears. Then the earth shook and quaked; the foundations of the mountains trembled; they shook because He burned with anger. Smoke rose from His nostrils,
and consuming fire came from His mouth; coals were set ablaze by it. He parted the heavens and came down, a dark cloud beneath His feet. He rode on a cherub and flew, soaring on the wings of the wind. He made darkness His hiding place, dark storm clouds His canopy around Him.
From the radiance of His presence, His clouds swept onward with hail and blazing coals.

The Lord thundered from heaven; the Most High projected His voice. He shot His arrows and scattered them; He hurled lightning bolts and routed them. The depths of the sea became visible, the foundations of the world were exposed, at Your rebuke, Lord, at the blast of the breath of Your nostrils. He reached down from heaven and took hold of me; He pulled me out of deep waters. He rescued me from my powerful enemy and from those who hated me, for they were too strong for me.

They confronted me in the day of my distress, but the Lord was my support. He brought me out to a spacious place; He rescued me because He delighted in me. The Lord rewarded me according to my righteousness; He repaid me according to the cleanness of my hands. For I have kept the ways of the Lord and have not turned from my God to wickedness. Indeed, I have kept all His ordinances in mind and have not disregarded His statutes. I was blameless toward Him and kept myself from sinning.

So the Lord repaid me according to my righteousness, according to the cleanness of my hands in His sight. With the faithful You prove Yourself faithful; with the blameless man You prove Yourself blameless; with the pure You prove Yourself pure, but with the crooked You prove Yourself shrewd. For You rescue an afflicted people, but You humble those with haughty eyes. Lord, You light my lamp; my God illuminates my darkness. With You I can attack a barrier, and with my God I can leap over a wall.

God—His way is perfect; the word of the Lord is pure. He is a shield to all who take refuge in Him.

For who is God besides Yahweh? And who is a rock? Only our God. God—He clothes me with strength and makes my way perfect. He makes my feet like the feet of a deer and sets me securely on the heights.

He trains my hands for war; my arms can bend a bow of bronze. You have given me the shield of Your salvation; Your right hand upholds me, and Your humility exalts me. You widen a place beneath me for my steps, and my ankles do not give way. I pursue my enemies and overtake them; I do not turn back until they are wiped out. I crush them, and they cannot get up; they fall beneath my feet. You have clothed me with strength for battle; You subdue my adversaries beneath me. You have made my enemies retreat before me; I annihilate those who hate me. They cry for help, but there is no one to save them—they cry to the Lord, but He does not answer them. I pulverize them like dust before the wind; I trample them like mud in the streets. You have freed me from the feuds among the people; You have appointed me the head of nations; a people I had not known serve me. Foreigners submit to me grudgingly; as soon as they hear, they obey me. Foreigners lose heart and come trembling from their fortifications. The Lord lives—may my rock be praised! The God of my salvation is exalted. God—He gives me vengeance and subdues peoples under me. He frees me from my enemies. You exalt me above my adversaries; You rescue me from violent men. Therefore I will praise You, Yahweh, among the nations; I will sing about Your name. He gives great victories to His king; He shows loyalty to His anointed, to David and his descendants forever.

God heard my cry that day. He reached down from heaven and rescued me from my enemies, for He knew they were too strong for me. God placed a wall of protection around me and my babies and as we flew home back to North Carolina. God told me that He delighted in me. He was proud of me for following Him and not turning to evil. He awarded me according to my righteousness. He rescued me from the violent man.

Chapter 3

"When you have nothing left but God, you will realize God is enough."
- Agnes Maude Royden

I remember the day that I told God "I surrender" all to Him. My life, myself, my kids, and my future. He put a song in my heart at that moment: "He's All I Need." That song played over and over in my head and peace replaced all the hurtful memories of my past. I knew that I had begun the healing process. I am so excited to tell you how God took over my life and played out His perfect plan from a simple prayer of total surrender.

After I came back to North Carolina, I moved in with my parents with only the clothes in my suitcase, $127 to my name, and my two kids. This is when I quickly realized that I had to completely rely on God. My heart was so full of joy, even though I had nothing. I *knew* that God was all I needed. I had the joy of my salvation in my heart and I felt His presence like never before. I was without a car, job, or money. But I *knew* that God was going to provide. With an open heart I stood back, listened, and waited for Him to move me.

I was able to get my car shipped to me from Arizona to North Carolina with the help of my parents. I then started applying for jobs. He offered no child support. I didn't care though; I wanted nothing from him.

I remember standing in line at the Department of Social Services applying for food stamps and insurance for my kids. I had never felt so low in my life. I was embarrassed. I was able to get assistance with food and insurance at this point, but I still needed a job. I had been a stay at home mom since my first child was born. I worked as a nursing assistant prior, which I let expire after becoming a stay at home mom. I had no idea what I was going to do!

As I sat in the Social Security office waiting for my name to be called, I looked around at all the others that were there needing assistance as well. They all looked sad, lonely, and desperate. Like me, they seemed broken. I stared at the door and wanted to make a run for it, to go back home and hide. Sure, I could have relied on my parents to provide for us, but that would have been selfish of me. I knew I had to be the adult and do whatever I could to provide for my kids.

After days and hours of job searching online and in newspapers, I felt led to go to a local staffing agency and apply for a job. I knew that God was in control, but the enemy also continued to attack me daily. I felt like the most insecure person in the world. I felt judged because I was going to be branded with the word "divorce." I felt unworthy of anything good happening to me. I had to be in constant prayer as I struggled with these insecurities. Little did I know, God was going to use those insecurities to build me some confidence!

This was my first test from God. During my interview at the staffing agency, we were going over my application and God said to me, "Say My name." He spoke so clearly that in that moment that I looked up to see who was speaking to me! My heart started racing. One thing that I struggled with in my faith was telling others about

God. This was so hard for me to do and now He wanted me to tell this lady His name! I started having this conversation with Him in my head and I said, "Ok, I'll do it, but when?!" I was freaking out at this point because I knew that my interview would soon be over. Then, God stepped in and set the perfect moment for me to mention His name. The lady asked, "What days will you be available to work?" Peace came over me at that moment and I said proudly, "Any day but Sunday; that day I want to set aside for God." She paused, stared at me for a moment, and smiled. She then said, "I have the perfect job for you, wait right here." She got up and walked around the corner. After a few minutes she came back and said, "I have you an interview set up for tomorrow morning at a doctor's office. I think you will fit in perfectly."

The next morning I went to my interview. It was for a medical assistant position at a doctor's office. I remember walking in and meeting with Sidney Carter (who would become one of my good friends) and Jackson Norton, the practice administrator (who would also become a good friend). I remember Jackson's first words, "We are a Christian organization." I felt God wrap His arms around me at that moment as He said to me, "I told you I will take care of you."

I got the job working for a wonderful doctor who taught me so much and with a company that encouraged me to keep down the path God had for me.

Wow! I did what God asked me to do and He provided!

When we are hurting, it's so important to surround ourselves with those that encourage us spiritually. This brings us closer to God and holds us accountable for our actions. God knew that I needed this and He knew that I needed Parkway Medical Group. I loved going to work and having my co-workers pray over me during my trials, as the following year I would go through the divorce and fighting for custody of my kids.

One of the exam rooms had a picture that hung on the wall of Jesus sitting in a chair and a little girl sitting on the floor at His feet with her head in his lap. At the bottom of the picture it said, "I will never fail thee." On days that I felt overwhelmed, I would walk into that exam room, look at the picture, and imagine that I was that little girl and that Jesus was speaking those words to me: "I will never fail thee."

I have learned to hold on to those special moments where God speaks to you. That picture now hangs in my house and serves as a reminder that God did not fail me. I knew my trials were not over yet.

I became involved in church and was asked to serve in children's ministry. I knew that this was God opening a door for me. He made it clear that it was important for me to serve in church.

After several months of teaching those precious kids, I was asked to write skits for large group. I found myself arguing with God the next day in the shower about writing these skits. "God, I'm not a writer! What am I going to do?!" At that moment, in the shower, God poured a skit into my heart. Not just a few lines, but the whole skit! He made it clear that if He calls me to do something, He will put the words in my mouth and the thoughts in my head, and He will provide the way. I am His vessel. I am being used by God to reach His world and He will use me the way He wants, as long as I have a willing heart. He will not call me to do His work without providing me with what I need to complete the task He has set before me.

Boy, did He bless me with those kids! I even witnessed my son accept Jesus into his heart. God was taking over my life and revealing Himself to me daily.

Chapter 4

"Faith is not thinking He can. It's knowing He will."
-Ben Stein

'Trust in the Lord with all your heart, and do not rely on your own understandings; think about him in all your ways, and He will guide you on your right paths." (Proverbs 3:5-6, HCSB)

The above verse is one of my favorite promises of God. Having faith in Him gave me the confidence that I needed to press on, take chances, and challenge myself in my daily tasks.

After God provided me with a job, I felt He was encouraging me to provide a home for me and my kids. "Trust Me," He would say. I am so thankful for the support from my family. They were right by my side the entire time, encouraging me and helping me in any way they could.

I started giving 10% of my paycheck to church. I'll never forget the feeling of joy when I received my first paycheck. I could not wait until Sunday so I could write that check and place it in the offering plate as it passed by me. I knew it was God's money. I knew it was the job God gave me and I knew what I had to do. The Bible tells us a few things about tithing and the promises that come with it.

Genesis 14:18-20 (HCSB) tell us, "Then Melchizedek, king of Salem, brought out bread and wine; he was a priest to God Most High. He blessed him and said: Abram is blessed by God Most High, Creator of heaven and earth, and I give praise to God Most High who has handed over your enemies to you. And Abram gave him a tenth of everything."

Not only did God give Abram a nation, He also blessed him and his 90-year-old wife, Sara, with a son! God blesses those who are faithful. Abraham and Sarah's son Jacob also tithed to God saying, "If God will be with me and watch over me on this journey, if He provides me with food to eat and clothing to wear, and if I return safely to my father's house, then the Lord will be my God. This stone that I have set up as a marker will be God's house, and I will give to You a tenth of all that You give me" (Genesis 28:20-22, HCSB).

In Numbers 18, the Lord commanded the Israelites to tithe ten percent of their earnings to the Lord. God then gave the tithes to support the Levites and Priests.

Let's look at Malachi. This was really an eye opener for me! In Malachi 3:8 (HCSB), God tells Malachi, "Will a man rob God? Yet are you robbing Me!" You ask: "How do we rob You?" By not making the payments of the tenth and the contributions." I knew I did not want to rob God of what was His!

But listen to this: verses 10-11 (HCSB) says, "'Bring the full tenth into the storehouse so that there may be food in My house. Test me in this way.' says the Lord of Hosts. 'See if I will not open the floodgates of heaven and pour out a blessing for you without measure. I will rebuke the devourer for you, so that it will not ruin the produce of your land and your vine in your field will not fail to produce fruit,' says the Lord of Hosts."

Here was my blessing from my faithful giving. I was at work one day and met someone who happened to work for Billy Graham.

I had a family member who also worked for Mr. Graham and we made the connection. He then asked if I was interested in working part-time for Mr. Graham as one of his caregivers. Wow, I was not expecting that! So, I applied for the job and was hired. I will never forget the first day I drove up to his house. What a blessing! Seeing him for the first time was indescribable. You could see a glow around this man as if God Himself placed it there (which I am sure He did). What an amazing experience to meet this man and serve him.

I will never forget talking to Mr. Graham about my five-year-old son. God had been dealing with his young five-year-old heart. Hunter, my son, would constantly talk about wanting to become a Christian. I was concerned that he was too young to fully understand. Mr. Graham told me, "He will know when it's his time, God will tell him." Such a sweet memory.

I had always wanted to meet Mr. Graham. I smile today thinking of how God allowed this circumstance to happen. It was as if He was saying, "Follow me and I will grant the desires of your heart."

After looking for only a few days, I found an apartment and was put on a waiting list. I was told it could take up to a month. I saved what I could, but with all the move in expenses plus first month's rent and deposit, I became worried. But my God proved to me that He was bigger.

I received a call saying an apartment was available a few days after turning in my application, and I could pick up the keys that week! I picked up my paycheck from my part time job with Mr. Graham. It was enough to cover all my move in expenses, what a blessing! Walking through that door for the first time was so humbling. Never did I imagine this could happen for me. God was pouring out His blessings for me and taking care of my family like He promised in Malachi.

But, my little 700-square-foot two-bedroom apartment was empty. We had clothes, food, and one twin bed. Our first night we ate pizza on the floor where a kitchen table would be. I didn't have much, but I felt like the richest person in the world.

The next day, I received a phone call from a friend. She had furniture she wanted to give me. We borrowed my parents' small flatbed trailer and drove to her house. On the way back, I got another phone call, and another.

That day I furnished my entire apartment with furniture that people gave me. I never had too much of one thing but just the right amount. I knew that was God providing yet again. God is so good and He will provide if you are faithful to Him with your tithes.

Jesus also teaches us that we are to be a cheerful giver. I knew that God had given me my job and I was so excited to give Him a tenth of my paycheck. God showed me this story in the Bible during that time. This was the kind of giver He wanted me to be.

Mark 12:41-44 (HCSB) tells the story of a beautiful temple filled with rich, elegant people that came to worship. "Sitting across from the temple treasury, He watched how the crowd dropped money into the treasury. Many rich people were putting in large sums. And a poor widow came and dropped in two tiny coins worth very little. Summoning His disciples, He said to them, 'I assure you: This poor widow has put in more than all those giving to the temple treasury. For they all gave out of their surplus, but she out of her poverty has put in everything she possessed — all she had to live on.'"

That is the heart I want to have when giving my tithes and offerings. God will live up to His promise. I am that proof of that, and you can be too. Be a cheerful giver and trust God with your finances, after all, He is the one that gave you that money!

This was just the beginning of God providing for me and my kids.

Chapter 5

Why Does God Allow Certain Things in Our Lives to Happen?

Fighting for custody of my kids brought my ex back to North Carolina. During our first court date, I was brought back to the state of panic and fear I had felt the day I left Arizona. "God, please protect my kids from this man." I knew the kind of person he was and so did God. My family came for support and many prayers were being sent.

The judge then allowed him to have supervised visitations with the kids. I was in shock. Why would God let this happen? He knows this man's heart! I was physically sick and wanted to take my kids and run. I called out to God, and He calmed my fears as He filled me with His peace.

I trusted his family at the time and they spent a few hours with the kids at Chuck E. Cheese supervising the visit. Handing my kids over to my mom and sister as they took them to meet my ex and his family was one of the hardest things I have ever done as a parent. A few hours later, they would be back safe with me. The court said I was the one assaulted but because the kids were not physically harmed, they felt it was ok for him to see the kids as long as the visits were supervised.

A few weeks passed after that visit and silence. No one called requesting another visit. I was so confused at this point and thought that maybe this was finally over.

That next visit never happened. A month later, I received a call from someone who wishes to remain anonymous telling me that he was in the hospital. He had assaulted another woman shortly after the visit with the kids and then attempted to commit suicide. He was in ICU for a month and then transferred to a mental hospital.

Thank you, God, for getting us out when you did! That could have been me or one of my kids. I was being told this in secret because his family had decided to hide this from me. Again, my heart was broken and I felt betrayed. I knew at this point I could no longer trust his family.

I was now on a mission. With the little information I had, I drove one hour to his hometown and went to every police station in the area looking for police reports. I was able to get pictures of the woman's face he had assaulted after she was sent to the hospital. My heart broke for her as I studied the image of her beaten, bruised and swollen face. She was unrecognizable.

I had copies of the arrest reports and sent them to my lawyer. My lawyer wanted us to reconcile and share custody, so I fired her and hired another lawyer. My new lawyer was able to get hospital records, police reports, and everything we needed to use against him in court. I wondered why God let him have that visit with the kids and why He allowed the court date to be continued. God was giving me evidence to prove my kids were not safe with him. After he was released from the hospital, the new court date was set. I also communicated with his probation officer back in Arizona and faxed papers of his arrest since he was on probation. A warrant was taken out for his arrest in Arizona. He never returned to Arizona and because it was a misdemeanor, Arizona would not pay to have him transferred from North Carolina.

I'll never forget that court date. I was ready to fight for my kids with all I had. My lawyer fought hard and in the end I was given full custody. He was awarded supervised visits with a therapist, who then would decide if he was fit to be involved in the lives of my kids.

Again, my heart was torn. "God, you delivered us from this man! You know his heart! You know how dangerous he is! Why? Why would you hand your precious children over to Him?" I thought we had enough proof to end this once and for all. The enemy tried to use this opportunity to turn me away from God. Although my heart was broken, my faith was not shattered. I knew this fight was not over and I needed to hold on tight to God's promises. He promised He would never fail me and I had to believe that.

We often wonder why God allows certain things to happen. We know in our hearts that He is working things out for our good and His purpose, but what does that look like in today's world? I'm going to tell you how He worked out my circumstance.

Fighting for my kids seemed like a never-ending battle. I was willing to do whatever it took to keep them safe, but it was out of my control now and I had to submit to the court system.

Psalm 46:1-2a says, "God is our refuge and strength, a helper who is always found in times of trouble. Therefore we will not be afraid."

I remember the day I drove the kids to meet with the therapist and my ex for their first session. My heart was pounding so hard I thought it was going to beat out of my chest. I knew had to trust God at this point; I had to believe. God carried me through that day. My kids were taken into a room with this man while I waited in another room. My emotions were everywhere! I wanted to hear my kids scream for me and yell at this man, but neither happened.

I taught my kids to pray for and forgive this man for the horrible memories they will always remember. I realized that I had taught them to do the things that I could not do myself.

I knew that I needed to forgive him. I tried, but at that time I just couldn't. I felt that justice was not being served and he was getting away with so much. I wanted him locked away forever, I wanted him to suffer for what he did to us. Forgiveness is so hard when someone hurts you or someone you love.

It took a while before I truly forgave him. I had a lot more healing to do myself before I was able to forgive. The enemy kept reminding me of things he did to me in the past. During my time alone I found that the enemy attacked me the most, so I tried to keep from being alone. I ran from the fear that I needed to face. God told me I needed to pray for this man. It was through my prayers that I found forgiveness. It was not easy, but the reward was peace. Oh, how I needed peace.

My son cried when I told him we had to go back to the therapist after that visit. I knew I had to keep fighting. I called the therapist and explained to her how my son felt after that visit. I then took him to meet with the therapist alone and she listened as he told her all his memories of that day. The gun, the couch pushed against the door so we could not leave, all the events of that day stored in my sweet boy's head that I pray will soon be forgotten.

But you know what? My God is good and He is so merciful!

After that visit with my son, the therapist ended all future visitations and told my ex that it was not therapeutic for him to be around my kids, ever.

It was finished! Yes, I had to suffer for a while, but God kept His promise. I just had to believe. We were finally free from this man!

Little did I know that God had orchestrated these events. He knew one day in the future I would need every detail of this long, exhausting, emotional journey. This story does not stop here, and I will need every bit of this proof God provided for a very special day to come.

His promises are true. Hold fast and believe His word. He proved His word true to me and I am so thankful. His path is not easy at times, but His strength will allow you to face the impossible. If you find yourself in the middle of a storm, trust Him. Believe His promises and pray them out loud. Remember where your strength comes from. Jesus is anxiously waiting for you to come to Him. During my trials and tribulations, I would remind myself of the song He placed on my heart, "He is all I need." Peace came as I sang out those words to God. Tell God today that He is all you need and I pray that you experience His peace in your heart. Remember, my friend, you are not alone and He will never fail you.

Chapter 6

"I have to believe."
-Rita Springer

I was in the seventh grade when I knew that I wanted to be a nurse. My ex was a nurse and he never encouraged me to go back to school. If fact, he would discourage me. He loved to feel in control and would tell me that I was not smart enough. After you hear that for so long, you start to believe it.

While working at Parkway Medical Group, I made some wonderful friends. One day at work, a friend and I were talking about going back to school and she started telling me about a school that just started a nursing program. Faye became one of my best friends and is still a special friend to me. I mentioned this program to another friend I worked with and he encouraged me to go apply and sign up for classes. He would not take no for an answer. He just kept on me so finally I went to apply for the nursing program. I worked during the day, and four nights a week I was at school until nine at night, then I drove home and studied until midnight.

I remember thinking, "What have I done? I will never be able to pull this off!" Yes, it was exciting, but I was not guaranteed into the nursing program and what would happen if I was accepted? Also, I would not be able to work, so how would I provide for my kids?

God spoke these precious words to my heart, "I can do all things through Christ who strengthens me" (Philippians 4:13, NKJV). As God filled my heart with this verse, He would say to me,

"I have brought you this far and provided for you, yet you still lack faith?" Then I had to surrender to Him all over again.

I knew I had to believe. I moved into my apartment, worked full time, went to school at night, and raised two kids. God carried me through this time. Looking back, I could not have done this without Him!

At the end of the year I finished all my prerequisites for the nursing program and it was time to take the placement test. I was competing with several others to get into the program and I was scared to death. They only took the top 30 scores.

I got a letter two days after Christmas. I had been accepted into the program! God said, "See, I told you so." I will never forget that feeling as I sat in my car reading that letter and crying tears of joy. God is so faithful!

I had another desire in my heart also, but I pushed it aside. I felt ashamed and unworthy to ask God of this, but He knew my desire and He knew my heart. I desired the kind of love that I had never known on this earth: true love. I knew this had to be His will if I ever had another relationship. I was not too hopeful, though. I remember telling God, "I give this to you, I surrender this desire of my heart. If it's not your will, please take away this desire." I was prepared to relinquish my hope of love. I put that desire at the feet of Jesus that day.

If you get a chance, listen to the song "I Have to Believe" by Rita Springer. During my times of uncertainty, I would sing this out to God. Such a powerful song! I pray it gives you the strength to press through whatever you are facing today. I love you, my friend, and so does your Heavenly Father who is always with you.

Chapter 7

"Be still and know that I am God." (Psalm 46:10a, NKJV)

"I waited patiently for the Lord, and He turned to me and heard my cry for help. He brought me up from a desolate pit, out of the muddy clay, and set my feet on a rock, making my steps secure. He put a new song in my mouth, a hymn of praise to our God. Many will see and fear and put their trust in the Lord. How happy is the man who has put his trust in the Lord and has not turned to the proud or to those who run after lies! Lord my God, You have done many things — Your wonderful works and Your plans for us; none can compare with You. If I were to report and speak of them, they are more than can be told. You do not delight in sacrifice and offering; You open my ears to listen. You do not ask for a whole burnt offering or a sin offering. Then I said, "See, I have come; it is written about me in the volume of the scroll. I delight to do Your will, my God; Your instruction lives within me." I proclaim righteousness in the great assembly; see, I do not keep my mouth closed — as You know, Lord. I did not hide Your righteousness in my heart; I spoke about Your faithfulness and salvation; I did not conceal Your constant love and truth from the great assembly. Lord, do not withhold Your compassion from me; Your constant love and truth will always guard me. For troubles without number have surrounded me; my sins have overtaken me; I am unable to see. They are more than the hairs of my head, and my courage leaves me. Lord, be pleased to deliver me; hurry to help me, Lord. Let those who seek to take my life be disgraced and confounded. Let those who wish me harm be driven back and humiliated. Let those who say to me, "Aha, aha!" be horrified because of their shame. Let all who seek You rejoice and be glad in You; let those who love Your salvation continually say, "The Lord is great!" I am afflicted and needy; the Lord thinks of me. You are my helper and my deliverer; my God, do not delay." (Psalm 40, HCSB)

I love being able to read the Bible and have a moment of, "Wow! That's exactly how I feel!" It's as if God wrote this passage just for me. The words then become my prayer. As I continue read His word, my heart rejoices as I feel Him draw close to me.

Sometimes, our trials are so great that we don't know how to put our feelings of despair into words. God understands our worries and doubts. He understands our hurt and our pain. He lives in us, feels our every emotion, and sees every tear. He knows every fear and every struggle. We are not alone.

God gave us His Spirit to live in us and to pray for us during those times of need. The Holy Spirit provides a way to communicate the words to pray when we are so overwhelmed that we can't even think. I remember the overwhelming fear as I sat in the courtroom waiting to hear the fate of my precious children. I remember the fear as I had my life threatened and was told to kiss my kids goodbye as a gun stared back at me. I remember the fear as I boarded that plane, heading over a thousand miles away from the control that I endured for seven years. I remember the fear of seeing the same vehicle he drove pass me on the road thinking he was coming after me. I remember not being able to come up with the words to pray in these times. All I could do was whisper His sweet name, "Jesus, Jesus."

I also remember the fear of the unknown as I sat in my tiny apartment balancing my checkbook and wondering how in the world was I supposed to provide for me and my kids and be a full-time student when on paper it seemed impossible.

Romans 8:26 (HCSB) says, "In the same way the Spirit also joins to help in our weakness, because we do not know what to pray for as we should, but the Spirit Himself intercedes for us with unspoken groanings."

Even though I feared failure, my God continued to say to me, "I am God. I am all you need. Let Me take care of EVERYTHING just as I always have when you have allowed Me to."

Looking back, God knew I struggled with trust and He knew He had to keep proving Himself to me. I'm so thankful He never gave up on me. With every door He opened, every word He spoke, and every fear He calmed, He would bring me through another storm. With each storm, He would eventually break down my wall piece by piece and my trust in Him grew stronger with each trial.

My friend, God is not going to give up on us! He will do whatever it takes to prove His love for us. He knows our heart better than we do. His love is unconditional and there is nothing that can separate His love from us, no matter what we have done in our past. My prayer for you is that you will live out that promise today.

My kids didn't have an earthly father at this time, but I made sure they knew they had a heavenly Father. What a perfect opportunity to point my kids to Christ! I saw a desire to know Jesus further grow in their hearts. Single moms, do not be discouraged if your child doesn't have an earthly father; point them to their heavenly Father. Tell them how He loves them and will protect them. Teach them how to pray to Him. Help them build a relationship with Jesus and watch the emptiness of their heart be filled with joy as they become confident in Christ. Ask God how to raise them up according to His will. I prayed this prayer many times and still do as they are now entering their teenage years. Trust God with your kids; after all, they are His children too.

I felt God's unconditional love through a sweet friend that God placed in my life. I felt he was always looking out for me. He was the one that encouraged me to start school and challenged me with my faith. I never thought of him as more than a friend until our friendship grew stronger. I knew he was the perfect guy, but probably not for me. I felt he deserved better. He was younger, single, and had a strong heart for God. He deserved someone just like him. I felt a certain peace about our friendship. I put our friendship in God's hands and was excited to have him as my best friend for the rest of my life if that was to be God's will.

Well, God had different plans, and little did I know, God was preparing this sweet, wonderful man's heart for something more than a friendship. He would soon embark on this crazy journey with me.

Before Brant and I started dating, I met with my pastor's wife to discuss my fears. Is this relationship accepted in the eyes of God? Am I free to be in a romantic relationship? I needed Godly counsel. After meeting with the sweet and precious Tracey and receiving her godly wisdom, I felt God's confirmation telling me it was ok to love and be loved by this man. It's so important to seek Godly counsel when you are unsure about anything in this life. This sweet lady was a wonderful mentor to me and I felt safe with her.

This sweet man would become my babysitter, my personal shopper, my maid, my personal tutor, and my encourager. He did these things with a smile on his face and never once complained. Brant Taylor knew how to be Jesus to me.

I struggled daily with the shame of being divorced. Divorce is such an ugly word. I felt like I had a scarlet letter stamped on me and felt as if the world was judging me. Brant never once judged me. He never once made me feel like I was less of a person. He showed me how one is supposed to love and how Jesus commands us to love - unconditionally.

Chapter 8

"When we put God first, all other things fall into their proper place or drop out of our lives."
-Ezra Taft Benson

God's love is so perfect. I think of my own children and how hard it must have been for God to have His only son die for us. I know I could never allow my child to die for anyone, especially for people that would not be grateful for their sacrifice. God showed us a love that no other love can compare to.

During my times of loneliness, I poured my time and energy into His word and prayer. God opened my heart to His pain and spoke so clearly to me, "I know your loneliness, I feel it every time I sit and wait for you to come spend time with me." Talk about an eye opener! I know the emptiness in my heart I feel when I go days without seeing my own children and how I long to hold them and feel their tiny arms wrap around me as they shower me with hugs and kisses. God made it clear to me that He craves that same affection from me. After all, He *is* our father. God also commands us to love others the way He loves us.

I remember the time I met Brant's family. Boy, was I nervous! I was a single mom, divorced with kids, and here I was dating this man six years younger than me. He comes from a wonderful family where most of the men are in ministry. I was so afraid of rejection, but God put a peace in my heart I that cannot describe.

This wonderful family not only welcomed me into their lives, but my two children as well. They loved us as their own. Brant's parents, sisters, aunts, uncles, grandparents and cousins never once made me feel as if I was not good enough.

What a perfect example of how Jesus taught us to love! They taught me the true meaning of unconditional love. Of course, the enemy constantly told me I was not good enough and Brant deserved better. But Brant stood up for his love for me in a way I had never experienced, even though I felt so unworthy.

Jeremiah 29:11 (HCSB) says, "'For I know the plans I have for you' — this is the Lord's declaration — 'plans for your welfare, not for disaster, to give you a future and a hope.'" I believe that our hearts need to be in the right place before God chooses to send that special someone. We first have to realize something bigger.

Luke 12:34 (HCSB) says, "For where your treasure is, there your heart will be also." Make God the treasure of your life and your relationship with Him your highest priority because "What eye did not see and ear did not hear, and what never entered the human mind —God prepared this for those who love Him." (1 Corinthians 2:9).

For those that have the same desire I had of true love, your heart must be completely in love with Jesus before He will reveal the one that He has chosen for you. The reason is that loving someone can turn into an idol. We can so easily take that love and allow it to consume our thoughts and our lives so much that we forget about Jesus. Jesus should be the true love we desire. By having this attitude, He will reward you with the desires of your heart if it's according to His will. This is the beautiful part: His will becomes your will when you truly love and follow Him.

Brant and I, along with the kids, drove to Louisiana to visit his parents. We had been dating for a while now, and I knew in my heart this man was someone I wanted to spend the rest of my life with. One afternoon, while we were in Louisiana, he took me out to dinner. He pulled into a nail salon and paid for me to have a manicure. He was always doing sweet things like that to make me feel special.

After my manicure, we headed to eat at California Pizza Kitchen. In my mind, I kind of thought that he was going to propose, but once we arrived to eat pizza, I was not convinced this was it. This place was not romantic at all, so I pushed the thought out of my head. After we ate, we walked around and visited nearby shops and he said he wanted to buy me a dress. I looked in several boutiques and after not really finding anything my style, I tried to convince him I did not need a dress. He was very adamant about me getting a dress, so I finally found one. It was still early and we had only been out for about an hour. He looked at his phone and he told me his mom was making his favorite dessert, Mississippi mud cake, and she was going to text him when she put it in the oven so we could hurry back. Really? Oh, I was getting mad. Here we were, on a date night and he could not wait to get home to eat his favorite dessert! Once I picked out my dress, he said, "OK, she put it in the oven so now we have to leave so by the time we get back it should be done!" I don't think I had ever been so mad at him!

I don't remember saying much on the ride back, but I do remember his excitement that he so openly displayed as we rushed back to his parents so he could eat his stupid Mississippi mud cake.

His mom met us at the front door and immediately wanted to see my dress. As I pulled the dress out of the bag, she was so excited and wanted me to go upstairs and try it on. Her excitement made me excited to try on this dress, so I hurried upstairs to change. As I started to come down the stairs, I looked down and saw Brant standing at the bottom. He had changed his clothes as well and looked so handsome in his tie.

He looked so nervous and I was so hoping that what I was thinking was true! At that moment, I forgot I was mad at him over the cake and my heart started pounding as I walked down the stairs, although in the back of my mind I wanted to turn around and run back into the bedroom, put on makeup, fix my hair, and put on shoes! But what the heck, I had my nails done and that was good enough for me.

He took my hand and led me to the screened-in porch. I remember walking through the kitchen thinking, "It's awful quiet in here." All the lights were out, and then he led me to the porch, and candles and roses were everywhere! I sat down in a chair as he pulled out a letter and started to read to me. He had music playing in the background and as he finished the letter, he got down on one knee and pulled out a beautiful ring! If I could have picked out my own ring, this was the one I would have chosen. He asked me to marry him, and of course I said yes! What made it even more special was after he proposed, he walked back inside, brought my two kids out on the pouch and explained to them what he did. The fact that he included my two children in that moment made it even more special to me. That night could not have been more perfect! We were then greeted back inside with his wonderful parents and two sisters who would soon become my sisters. What a night, what a blessing, and what an amazing God.

Five months later, we were married. We had the most amazing wedding. After we walked down the aisle, my daughter walked up to Brant and said, "I love you, Daddy." He had told them after we were married they could call him "Daddy." We were now a family.

Chapter 9

To All the Single Ladies

Are you single and looking for "Mr. Right"? Are you heartbroken, worried, or confused about a current relationship? Are you fed up? Done? Finished with relationships?

I remember that feeling as well when I was 19. I was tired of waiting. I was so tired of waiting that I turned my back on God. Instead of waiting for the one He had chosen for me, I chose for myself. Boy, was I ever wrong.

Sure, I thought I had found "the one." But deep in my heart I knew God was telling me "no." I prayed for God to bless my decision anyway.

Seven years of abuse was waiting for me just around the corner. Seven years of hurt, betrayal, lies, disappointments, and fear, all from my selfish desire.

I finally turned back to God. God delivered me from this man and I am here to tell you of the perfect love that no man on this earth can give us. Search no more for a man to fill that void in your life, because He is here.

Let's look at what the Bible says about His perfect love:

"The Lord has appeared of old to me, saying: 'Yes, I have loved you with an everlasting love; Therefore with lovingkindness I have drawn you.'" (Jeremiah 31:3, NKJV)

"Yet in all these things we are more than conquerors through Him who loved us. For I am persuaded that neither death nor life, nor angels nor principalities nor powers, nor things present nor things to come, nor height nor depth, nor any other created thing, shall be able to separate us from the love of God which is in Christ Jesus our Lord." (Romans 8:37-39, NKJV)

God said to me one day, "Sometimes you run from me and my plans for your life. Just know I will always be waiting for you to come back. My plans for you will always be available whenever you are ready for it. I will not love you any less for choosing your own way. But just know that I have such great things in store for you, because I do know your future, I AM the one who made you, and all things work out for those who love and follow Me. I loved you so much that I allowed my only son to be nailed to the cross for you so you can be forgiven."

I have found that His plan for my life is so much better than my plan I had chosen. There is no man on this earth that can love me as much as God. He fills my heart with joy, He makes my loneliness disappear, and He speaks to me daily to remind me He is with me. I am NEVER alone!

I never thought I would get married again, much less find someone that would love me AND my kids. In my mind, I was going to be a single mom for the rest of my life. And my heart was content with that because my relationship with Christ grew so strong that He filled that emptiness in my heart. But He also left the desire.

I am excited to tell you that God gave me that desire. The

sweetest thing about this man is that God sent him to me; He had all this planned out. I don't know if we would have ended up together if I had chosen to stay in God's will for my life the first time, but I do know that God was waiting for me to come back to Him. He wrapped His loving arms around me and pointed me in His direction, which led me to Brant Taylor's heart. Then He carefully orchestrated the events which led to Brant adopting Hunter and Kayla and protected us from evil, not to mention preparing my heart and mind to go back to school at thirty years old to follow my dream of becoming a nurse.

My point is, we dream as little girls about our wedding day, about the man that we are to spend the rest of our lives together with, and one day having a family of our own. We sometimes become impatient when it doesn't happen when we want it to. We wonder why God has not sent "the one" yet but has sent all of our friends their "chosen one." Please listen to God on this one, girls. Trust me, He knows what He is doing! Don't settle for the first one that comes along because you are tired of waiting. Pray and ask God to show you His plan for your life. And if He makes it clear that it's not with the guy you are dating, get out. He has someone better for you. Here is one of my favorite quotes from Maya Angelou: "A woman's heart should be so hidden in Christ that a man should have to seek Him first to find her."

Chapter 10

*"On the day I called, You answered me; You increased
strength within me." (Psalm 138:3, HCSB)*

Do you ever stop and think of how you wish you could have
done something different in your life? Do you ever wish you would
have taken a different career path, or took that leap of faith and
pursued your dream? Do you ever feel like it's too late? Do you
think to yourself, "I don't have time for this," "I'm not smart
enough" or "I just can't"? What we need to understand is that God
can! Jesus says in Mark 9:23b (HCSB), "Everything is possible to
the one who believes."

I had those same thoughts when I started pursuing my
nursing career. I had always wanted to be a nurse since I was in
seventh grade. I was so overwhelmed with joy and fear at the same
time as I read those unforgettable words telling me I had been
accepted into the nursing program. The devil tried to take that joy
and tell me that I was not going to succeed, that I was going to fail. I
prayed hard and God gave me the confidence and strength I needed.

I love the sweet words that He whispered in my heart during
that time: "I can do all things through Christ who gives me strength"
(Philippians 4:13, NKJV).

I studied like I had never studied before. God put confidence
in me as I worked for Him. "Whatever you do, do it enthusiastically,
as something done for the Lord and not for men" (Colossians 3:23,
HCSB).

Yes, I struggled daily with believing I was not smart enough. After someone tells you that for so long, you start to believe it. But through prayer, God continued to encourage me. "On the day I called, You answered me; You increased strength within me" (Psalm 138:3, HCSB).

Before we were married, my sweet Brant would come over and keep the kids while I studied. He cleaned my apartment, made sure we had food to eat, and even helped out with the bills. I was so blessed to have him. God, Brant, and chocolate chip cookies helped me through nursing school. I waited until the kids went to bed and baked cookies for myself. If you are a parent, I'm sure you have done this before and I know you understand. I got away with it for a while until I left the pan on the stove and the kids eventually caught on.

With three months left of school, Brant and I married and he moved in our tiny apartment. We were cramped, but we were happy. We didn't have much, but we had each other. I was happy and the joy of my salvation flowed through my heart. Looking back, I often miss that time. It was in those moments of not having much where I felt the closest to God. He showed me that He was all I needed. Nothing in this world could satisfy my heart the way He did.

I graduated nursing school, and two weeks later I passed the NCLEX. I became Stacie Taylor, RN. God continued to amaze me. I was sitting in my car waiting to go to my pinning ceremony, and my phone rang. I got a job offer with the hospital I did my preceptorship with. God is so good! I gladly accepted my first nursing position. I have no doubt God had a hand in that. There is nothing impossible for God! He has opened so many doors for me and I am so overwhelmed with His blessings. I felt so unworthy of all these blessings. All this was from a simple surrender, but not just any surrender, a total surrender.

God put me in a job that He knew was the right fit for me. It was a small hospital and I made some lifelong friendships. Everyone in the hospital became family to me, and it was full of the most encouraging people I had ever met. I was so blessed to be a part of that family. My preceptor, Jennifer McDevit, became someone that would hold such a special place in my heart. She is such a strong woman of God and I am so thankful God placed her in my life. I learned so much from her and everyone I worked with. They all will forever hold a special place in my heart. God knew what He was doing when He placed me at that hospital.

During that time, Brant and I found a beautiful house to rent. I had a family, a home, a career of my dreams, a wonderful job; I was so blessed. I went to my job every day and worked as if I was working for God Himself.

After I had been at Transylvania Hospital for a year, I received a national nursing award (The Daisy Award) after one of my sweet co-workers, Beverly Hinkle, and a precious family I cared for nominated me. To a person who had little belief in herself, this sure gave me confidence! It is such a sweet memory I will never forget. Thank you, Beverly, for believing in me.

Total surrender is when you give your entire self to God. Start by reading His word daily. Stay in constant prayer while seeking Him out in times of trouble. Continually give thanks and obey His commandments while turning from sin. Love everyone the way He loves us, and do your work to the best of your ability to please Him and not man. Go where He tells you to go and trust Him with every detail in your life, even the tiny ones.

This definition of total surrender is not what I found in a book or copied from someone else; these are my words from my experiences. This is how I surrendered myself completely to Him.

Chapter 11

I am Weak, But He is Strong

I love those simple words we sang as a child: "Jesus loves me this I know, for the Bible tells me so, little ones to Him belong, they are weak but He is strong."

Think for a minute about the power of God. Some may find fear in His power, but my heart fills with an indescribable joy. He is my creator, my savior, and my Father; I belong to Him!

I can rest in peace knowing that He, the almighty creator of all things, powerful, never changing wonderful Father of mine, has His loving arms wrapped around me at all times. He lives in me, sees my every thought, and guides me and protects me at all times; not just in my times of trouble, but ALL the time.

"Don't worry about anything, but in everything, through prayer and petition with thanksgiving, let your requests be made known to God. And the peace of God, which surpasses every thought, will guard your hearts and minds in Christ Jesus." (Philippians 4:6-7, HCSB)

"And let the peace of the Messiah, to which you were also called in one body, control your hearts. Be thankful." (Colossians 3:15, HCSB)

"Devote yourselves to prayer; stay alert in it with thanksgiving." (Colossians 4:2, HCSB)

"Rejoice always! Pray constantly. Give thanks in everything for this is God's will for you in Christ Jesus." (1 Thessalonians 5:16-

18, HCSB)

The Holman Illustrated Bible Commentary describes worry in this way: "Worry is anxiety. Prayer is the antidote for worry." Now, listen to this: "Thanksgiving shapes prayers with gratitude. In response, the peace of God brings power to endure."

Worry, worry, worry, stress, more worry; this was so me! We all struggle with worry and stress. God made it so clear to me that if I would just trust Him, He would take all my worries away. This is easier said than done, right? I have learned that once I stop focusing on my worries and start giving thanks for my trials and surrender my control, the peace of God then fills my heart.

Brant and I had been married for six months, and at this point in my life, I was happy. God has blessed me more than I deserved. It had been over a year since we had any contact with my ex.

Brant and I knew it was time. I had to prepare myself; opening the wounds that had not completely healed was going to be hard. Yes, my wound would leave a scar, but that scar would be a reminder of God's power and unconditional love, a love that I would share with others who would see my scar. It would be a battle scar that He would use to show the world His love, mercy, forgiveness, and power. It would be a victory scar to show He won and the enemy lost.

Brant wanted Hunter and Kayla to be Taylors. He was prepared to do whatever it took and pay whatever amount to have my precious kids carry his name. We wanted our family to be complete, we wanted a new start.

After Brant and I were married, I would find papers in the kids' backpacks with the name Taylor written on them. My heart ached as I had to explain to them that my last name was Taylor, not theirs. They couldn't understand why my last name changed, but theirs didn't. They wanted to be Taylors so badly. We knew then what we needed to do. Brant was very determined to make this happen. His love for my kids amazed me. He always amazed me in everything he did. Thank you, God, for sending us this wonderful man.

North Carolina has very strict criteria for terminating parental rights. We knew we would be in for a fight, but it was a fight worth fighting for. Right after we met with our lawyer, paid our fee, and served my ex with papers, we found a new criminal conviction on his record. He had another arrest for domestic violence. I drove back down to his hometown, one hour away, and gathered all the police evidence I could. This poor woman was beaten and held hostage in his home.

Again, flashbacks flooded my mind and my heart broke for this woman. This was the second time he did this to her and I felt that I had failed her. I tried so hard to have him put away after he assaulted her the first time. He was released and she was pulled back into his trap. I found her on Facebook and asked her to testify against him in court, and I explained we were trying to have his rights terminated. No response.

I remember our first court date. Brant and I prayed before we left, since just knowing my ex could be in the same building brought fear over me. We stepped off the elevator and there he was, sitting on the bench with his dad. We had not heard from him, and my lawyer believed he would not show up. But there he was. My heart sank. I had to prepare for yet another fight, a fight I would do over and over for my kids. God continued to strengthen me in my weakness. This was the first time Brant had seen him. I almost wished Brant had not come. I knew it pained him to see this man. I wanted to protect Brant's heart, but he stayed by my side and never let go of my hand.

"Whoever sacrifices a thank offering honors Me, and whoever orders his conduct, I will show him the salvation of God." (Psalm 50:23, HCSB)

Chapter 12

"Consider it great joy, my brothers, whenever you experience various trials, knowing that the testing of your faith produces endurance." (James 1:2-3, HCSB)

God brought me to a place of peace. After carrying me this far in life, He knew I was ready for this trial. He was preparing me for this battle. At this point in my life I knew, without a doubt, that ALL things are possible with God, I can do ALL things through Christ who gives me strength, ALL things work out for the good of those who love Him, and He will calm ALL my fears and doubts. I knew that my prior trials produced endurance.

I opened my eyes one morning to the picture that hung on the wall in a place where it would be one of the first sights my eyes would focus on: the picture of Jesus with his arms wrapped around a scared little girl. The sweet, precious words would then fill my head and my heart: "I will not fail thee." I needed those constant reminders all day long. Whether it was a picture on the wall, a song I was listening to as I drove, or a verse written on my hand. I wanted and needed so desperately to feel His constant presence.

And when I didn't feel Him, depression, doubt, fear, and anxiety would step in. The enemy would slip these thoughts into my head. Every day was a struggle as I faced those demons. I found ways to stay close to God. I believe God allows you to go through trials in your life to make you stronger, as if He is preparing you for something greater. James 1:2-3 (above) explains that very well.

I love the book of James, and it is probably my favorite book in the Bible. Anyone who has experienced a lot of pain, loneliness, hurt, and confusion should read this book. This book brought me hope. I love James 1:1 (HCSB) where it says, "James, a slave of God and of the Lord Jesus Christ." That's who I want to be, a slave to my Heavenly Father.

Nothing in the world fills my heart with the kind of joy my Father brings. I love the joy I receive when I serve my Father. I can almost see Him smiling down at me saying, "That's my daughter." Oh, what a feeling! I want to live in His presence forever. That is my desire. I feel safe in His presence.

I was at work one day and a coworker was complaining about how the doctors think we, as nurses, should drop everything for them. She was clearly upset, and my response was, "We are here to serve." My heart broke when she replied, "I'm not their servant." She didn't get it, and my heart hurt for her. I know I was called to be a servant of Christ. Christ calls us to serve others, not just my patients but everyone in my life. Jesus tells us in Mark 9:35 (HCSB), "If anyone wants to be first, he must be last of all and a servant to all."

"Even as the Son of Man came not to be served but to serve, and to give his life as a ransom for many." (Mark 10:45, NKJV)

"For though I am free from all men, I have made myself a servant to all, that I might win the more." (1 Corinthians 9:19, NKJV)

Jesus tells us that He did not come to this world so He may

be served, He came to this world to serve. When I choose to serve others, I feel close to my Father. This feeling makes me homesick; I cannot wait to walk the streets of gold with my Father and never feel pain, hurt, depression, fear, or anxiety again.

Until that day comes, I am content knowing that I can live close to Him while I'm here on earth, and I am thankful that He gives me instructions through His Word on how to seek Him.

Brant and I sat patiently as we waited in the courtroom. My ex did not show up with a lawyer. Our lawyer was informed that he was going to ask for a court appointed lawyer to represent him. My heart sank as I was told this news.

But, as I looked up at Brant and saw his big, beautiful smile and the love in his eyes as he held my hand gently but tightly, my loneliness and fear faded away. I love it when God speaks to me through this man. Remembering that God's timing is perfect and looking back at how He revealed His plan so far leaves me speechless. He got us to this point and I can just imagine Him sitting back with a big smile on His face as He cannot wait to reveal to us the ending of this story!

The peace that filled the courtroom that day was simply amazing. My racing heart started to slow down, my breathing became normal, and my mind was calm. Brant felt the peace also. We had a lot of people praying for us that day and I know that when two or more people come together in prayer, God hears every word. I am a firm believer in prayer. "For where two or three are gathered in my name, there am I among them." (Matthew 18:20, HCSB)

My ex stood and the judge asked if he would like a court appointed lawyer. As he stood up, his disheveled appearance was trying to look confident and ready to fight, but as the presence of God filled the room, his expression changed and his entire demeanor changed as well. I knew in my heart God was convicting that man. He then tells the judge that he was tired of fighting and did not want a lawyer.

What?! Now my heart rate started increasing just a little, well maybe a lot. He looked confused and he was stumbling over his words. I witnessed the power of prayer firsthand that day. The enemy had lost. He was no match for my Father!

After he and his dad spoke briefly in the hallway to our lawyer, he agreed that he would be willing to sign over his rights if I would allow his family to continue to have contact with the kids. Brant and I agreed as we both felt peace about this decision. But, he needed proof before he would sign the papers. I had to prove to him that I would keep my word. I felt his control start to slip back over me.

"A man who endures trials is blessed, because when he passes the test, he will receive the crown of life that God promises to those who love Him." (James 1:12, HCSB)

God then tells my heart, "Serve them, love them." Brant and I invited his family, without him, to our home one Saturday shortly after the court date. We would spend most of the day together. They spent time with the kids, we ate, and we laughed. It was a good day. It was good for me to see them also. I had so many mixed emotions because they were like family to me and I feared their resentment. I was relieved that they were happy for me and the kids and did not blame me for my decisions. They were happy we had Brant.

Brant and I ended that day with hope, the hope that the adoption would soon be over. He was supposed to sign the papers that following Monday after his family came for a visit. Brant and I anxiously waited for that Monday to come. But Monday came and we heard nothing.

Chapter 13

"Wait for the Lord; be strong and courageous. Wait for the Lord." (Psalm 27:14, HCSB)

How many times have we been reminded to wait on God in our lifetime? How many times do we sit and wait for God to move or answer a prayer? How many times do we fear His answer? How many times do we wonder if He hears our cry?

God tells us, "Be anxious for nothing, but in everything by prayer and supplication, with thanksgiving, let your requests be made known to God" (Philippians 4:6, NKJV). Also, "Then He spoke a parable to them, that men always ought to pray and not lose heart," (Luke 18:1, NKJV).

Jesus taught us to pray, pray, pray and to not give up hope. God hears our prayers.

I remember the feelings of disappointment, hurt, betrayal, and confusion as Monday ended and we were left with nothing. His lawyer had not heard from him and we felt defeated. We were sure that it would be over.

Brant and I wanted God's will in this. We both understood that His will may not be for the kids to be adopted by Brant. We accepted this, surrendered this desire to the Lord, and waited.

Several weeks later, we scheduled another court date. This court date would be me giving my testimony to the judge, and the judge would then decide the fate of my children.

I knew God would prepare me and give me the strength I

needed. I knew that if this was what it took to protect my kids, I would be ready.

I rehearsed my testimony over and over in my head. The memories of my past were so painful and overwhelming. How much longer do I have to endure these memories? It was during this time that God opened my eyes to the fact that I had regressed so many of these memories and I was living in bondage of them. I had a long way to go before my wounds would heal. I thought I was completely healed, but I was wrong. God had me to open my wounds and from there I would start the healing process. God was telling me to write my story. I remember the excitement as I started writing this book.

I asked God, "What will the title be?" I quickly remembered that when He calls you to do something, He will equip you with all you need.

I woke up one morning with three words stuck in my head, repeating over and over: "Broken, wounded, healed, broken, wounded, healed, broken, wounded, healed...." God had given me the title of His story.

As I started writing out my testimony, God pointed out the areas where He was during my journey in life. I was amazed how He spoke to me through this. At one point during my writing I became so emotional that I couldn't continue. I remember sitting on the couch, crying as I relived my past.

I stopped writing for several weeks and felt the Holy Spirit constantly telling me to continue, so I opened up my laptop and started to type.

I felt His peace and understanding come over me as I relived these events and found myself with a strength that I had not felt before. I was ashamed of my past decisions. I had hurt stored in my heart from many others in my life. God brought peace and poured out His unconditional love over me.

What an amazing feeling it is to know the one who created me, loved me through my mistakes, and never left my side. I was the one that left His side. I was the one that chose my path and not His.

When I turned back to Him, He was waiting for me with open arms and chose to forget all my sins. No other love is greater than that. I found forgiveness in myself as God revealed His love for me as I wrote out my story. I now live with the hope of the future, and not the fear of my past.

If God allowed the adoption to take place on the first court date, I believe I would not have found this self-forgiveness.

The day before our next court date we received a phone call from our lawyer. My ex had called her personally and agreed to sign the papers at court the next day. He stood by his word this time and signed over his parental rights that next day.

Today, my sweet kids, Hunter and Kayla, are carrying the name Taylor. The enemy tried hard to keep this from happening and the adoption was postponed for several months due to missing paperwork, but my God is bigger and defeated him once again.

God was preparing for us to move away from North Carolina, and my heart broke as I had to say goodbye to my work family. Brant and I were both comfortable in our current jobs and we were so blessed to work in a Christian setting that encouraged our faith. But we both knew God did not want comfortable. He needed us to continue His work as we were being called to move.

We started applying for jobs in Tennessee, and I was called for an interview at a hospital in downtown Nashville. This was definitely out of my comfort level! I grew up driving on backroads and had never experienced big city traffic. On my way to my interview my sweet mother-in-law drove me downtown. I remember the fear and wondered if this was truly God's calling.

I sat in my interview that day and the peace of God came over me when I was asked why I wanted to be a nurse. My mind drifted back to my first interview where God said, "Say my name." He again told me at that moment, "Say my name." My response came much easier this time, "This is what God has called me to do."

Again, I saw God. I was hired on the spot. I went home and said goodbye to my family and friends and my husband. It was not a permanent goodbye to my husband, but only for a few months as he would finish his job in North Carolina.

The kids and I moved in with my in-laws and had the most wonderful experience that summer. God really blessed me with this family and I learned so much about my faith just by watching them. They are and always will be an inspiration to me, and I'm so excited to be able to learn from them as I grow as a mother, a wife, and a child of God.

A few months later, Brant moved to Tennessee and we bought our first home. I cannot deny for one second that God did this. God worked out His perfect plan for my life and now that I have learned to trust Him in all things, I get to live in His peace and not in my past.

God gets all the glory here, I am just His servant.

Chapter 14

Why Do Bad Things Happen?

"Why me?"

We have all asked that question. We have all told ourselves, "I'm not a bad person, why do bad things keep happening? When will this madness of life stop!?"

What I have come to realize is that this madness will end when we are sitting by the throne of God in our final resting place, for all eternity, at the feet of Jesus. Then, my friend, we rest.

I often tell myself, "Things are going good for me now, but I know this will not last." I become anxious about my next trial and allow this thought to almost paralyze me.

It's during this time that I long for my home, my heavenly home, and the joy that fills my heart when I think of my Jesus wrapping His arms around me and drying all my tears as He takes away all the pain of this world. What a day that will be! But until then, we are here in this world, in this place of pain and suffering. How do we live with the joy of our salvation? How do we keep that joy? How do we find the peace that God promises to us?

"Peace I leave with you. My peace I give to you. I do not give to you as the world gives. Your heart must not be troubled or fearful." (John 14:27, HCSB)

So here we are, my amazing husband and me and my two precious kids that have brought so much joy to my life, and a wonderful family and friends and our beautiful first home as a family, and I have my dream job. We have been blessed with a wonderful church family that we adore, and I have been blessed y'all! I get to go out and show Jesus to this world without a fear of being arrested; I am free! So why is life so hard after all God has blessed me and my family with? My lifetime of troubles were supposed to be over, right? I now follow Him completely. Doesn't that guarantee no future troubles? This is what the enemy wants us to believe so we will turn from God when things go bad.

God does not promise a day without troubles or a day without trials and tribulations, but we should have peace knowing that He is in control!

"These things I have spoken to you, that in Me you may have peace. In the world you have tribulation, but take courage; I have overcome the world." (John 16:33, NKJV)

That's why we need Him. That's why we are constantly searching for Him. This is why we need to stay in constant prayer. Trust Him to give us the strength we need to make it through our day. The difference of a believer in Christ and a non-believer is that we, as Christians, know we can't live in this world without the help of our Savior. I'm sure we all have, at some point in our lives, tried to live on our own. Those who choose to follow Christ come to realize it's much easier to let God take care of us than to do it on our own.

Brant and I had a miscarriage a few years after we were married. I was only eight weeks pregnant when we found out. I wanted that baby so badly! My heart was broken. Anyone who has experienced this knows the pain. How could God allow this bad thing to happen to me?

I questioned Him. I begged Him to make that tiny heart start beating before I had my procedure to remove the baby. I knew they would do another ultrasound prior to my procedure and I prayed so hard that we would see a heartbeat on that next ultrasound. I couldn't understand why this was happening. Why would God allow me to go through another trial so hurtful after all that He delivered me from?

This was a different pain than I had experienced before. This was a pain that I could not see anything good coming out of. My baby was dead. I went four days before I had my dilation and curettage (D&C) procedure and just knowing I was carrying a baby inside that was no longer living was one of the most painful experiences I have been through, and I have been through a lot of pain in my life. I didn't know how to respond to this. My past trials were painful, but this was a different kind of pain. I didn't understand how to deal with this pain, this grief.

One day I asked God how I was supposed to move on from this. This verse came to me: "Consider it great joy whenever you experience various trials, knowing that the testing of your faith produces endurance" (James 1:2-3, HCSB)

"Ok, yes Lord, but how am I supposed to have this joy? How am I supposed to respond to this? How do You want me to respond? I'm not finding this joy!"

I got up one morning a few weeks after my procedure. I fixed my breakfast and sat down for my quiet time. As I opened my Bible, the book of Job stood out to me. God was speaking to me. I knew Job had went through lots of trials and I first thought God was telling me that my trial was small compared to what this guy went through and I should stop complaining and get over this, but that's not God.

I started to doubt Him, and I let the enemy control my thoughts about my Father. I needed to be strong, suck it up, and get over it. That was how I was raised to deal with hurt and rejection, but God showed love to me in a different way, just as He always did when I doubted Him. He never gave up on me, even when I turned my back. That's what I love about my Father - His perfect, unconditional love that no one else in this world can show me.

Close your eyes for just a second and focus for a moment on this kind of love. Do you feel that? Do you feel the joy and excitement in your heart? Does that make you desire to be closer to Him and know Him more intimately? That desire is God calling out to you! He is the only one that can feel your heart with the kind of love that allows you to see things not of this world, but of Him.

God wanted to tell me something in the book of Job. I love that feeling when a verse or book of the Bible stands out to me and I know that God is wanting to tell me something. He wants to speak to me. I am so small in comparison to Him, I'm like a grain of sand on the beach, and He wants to personally talk to me!

For those that have not read Job, let me explain what this story is about. He was described as a "man of perfect integrity; who feared God and turned away from evil" (Job 1:1b, HCSB). Satan took away Job's family, home, and his animals; everything in Job's life was taken away and destroyed. Then Satan placed large boils all over Job's body. This man lost everything and suffered physically as well. Satan thought that Job would turn from God, but here is how Job responded: "The Lord gives and the Lord takes away, Praise the name of Yahweh (God). Throughout all this, Job did not sin or blame God for anything" (Job 1:21b-22, HCSB).

I knew at that moment how to respond to this pain that filled my heart. And at that moment, I fell to my knees and praised His holy name. What an amazing God we serve! God took the grief out of my heart that day. All I had to do was praise His name.

I thanked God for this trail, for it brought me and my husband closer. It opened my eyes to how I can go through life without living in fear. It brought me closer to God.

My first day back to work was hard, both physically and mentally. I trusted Him to get me through that day as I struggled holding back tears all day long. He knew I was struggling and He reached out to me.

I was asked to stop an IV pump by a nurse I worked with. As I walked in the patient's room, he had the sweetest smile on his face and was so thankful for the little act I did. He told me to pick up a puzzle in the bag by the door and take it with me. Not knowing what the puzzle was, I thanked him, took a bag filled with the little pieces and walked out. As I looked closely, I realized it was a cross puzzle that the patient had handmade. I knew that God orchestrated that moment. He reminded me that He was with me and reminded me that all I had to do was bring all my troubles to the cross. There I would find Him.

Oh, and for those who are wondering what happened to Job: "So the Lord blessed the last part of Job's life more than the first. He owned 14,000 sheep, 6,000 camels, 1,000 yoke of oxen, and 1,000 female donkeys. He also had seven sons and three daughters... Job lived 140 years after this and saw his children and their children to the fourth generation. Then Job died, old and full of days" (Job 42:12-13,16-17, HCSB).

This passage gave me hope. I cannot wait to see His plan for my life unfold. No matter what trial we are in or are about to be in, thank Him for it. Continue to praise His name and trust His will. He will not let you down. Nothing in this world can compare to His peace. I hope you know that peace.

Chapter 15

God Gives Us More Than We Can Handle

We have all heard the phrase, "God will never give us more than we can handle." I'm going to be real here and tell you that this is not true.

I'll never forget a hospice patient I had. I was giving her large doses of morphine every 5 minutes to try to make her comfortable, which was not working. I stood at her bedside, watching this poor woman struggling to breathe, drowning as her lungs filled with fluid, and yelling out in pain. Watching the family suffer through this was almost as unbearable. I was struggling to hold it together myself. This sweet lady was going through something so painful and terrifying that it was so hard to see God in this. I knew He put me in this position to care for this lady and her family. I knew I had to be Jesus to this precious lady and her family. Right before she took her last breath, her body relaxed and her eyes opened. She seemed to focus on something or someone, smiled, and took her last breath. Peace filled the room. We all knew her suffering had ended and she was with her Maker. I was so blessed to witness her last breath as she went home to be with Jesus. God showed Himself to me and her family that day and we left knowing that God is real.

"He gives strength to the weary and strength to the powerless. Youths may faint and grow weary, and young men stumble and fall, but those who trust in the Lord will renew their strength; they will soar on wings like eagles; they will run and not grow weary; they will walk and not faint." (Isaiah 40:29-31, HCSB)

The key phrase here is "those who trust in the Lord." What about those that don't believe in God? My heart breaks for them because they don't know this strength. Sometimes, we as believers suffer too.

As a Christian, I have been brought to my knees many times in my life. We allow this world to get in between our relationship with God and because of our free will, our sinful nature tempts us to look upon worldly things and forget about God.

When we take our eyes off Him, we fall. We are then quickly reminded that we lost our focus. God knows that, and He loves us anyway! He is always willing to forgive. I used to beat myself up pretty bad for the mistakes I have made in my past and not turning to God for direction, but He was always waiting for me with open arms ready to take me back. Now that is love!

I believe God allows certain circumstances to happen in our lives that can literally bring us to our knees.

Brant and I found out we were having a baby three months after my last miscarriage. After going through the miscarriage, I remember the grief and crying out to God asking "Why?" The grief lasted for months and I thought I would never heal. This brought me to my knees. God taught me that through any circumstance, no matter what happens, to trust in Him. Trust. It's so hard to do when you are in the middle of a storm. But when it's hard, lift up your hands to Him and say, "I will still worship Your name, Jesus." Oh, the peace it will bring. Once we decide that we need Him and come to that point in our lives, we allow God to take control, which is His desire. He wants to help us through these times, He wants to be our rock. He is anxiously waiting for us to turn to Him so He can pour out His strength in us so we know that we can do all things through Him.

Instead of saying God will never place anything on us we can't handle, I believe the correct phrase is: There is nothing too hard I that I can't handle if I hold tight to God. I couldn't find anything in the Bible that talks about God not giving us more than we can handle, but here is what I did find: strength.

"The Lord is my strength and my song; He has become my salvation. This is my God and I will praise Him, my father's God, and I will exalt Him." (Exodus 15:2, HCSB)

"I love You, Lord, my strength." (Psalm 18:1, HCSB)

"The Lord is the strength of His people;" (Psalm 28:8a, HCSB)

"God is our refuge and strength, a helper who is always found in time of trouble." (Psalm 46:1, HCSB)

"But those who trust in the Lord will renew their strength." (Isaiah 40:31, HCSB)

My precious mother-in-law called me after looking through her 2013 calendar. She asked me if I remembered what happened May 21, 2013. I had my D&C that day from my miscarriage. At our first ultrasound for our baby girl, her due date was May 21, 2014, although she ended up being born on May 14. Again, through this experience, I felt God wrap His loving arms around me as He reminded me that He is in control.

Chapter 16

I am My Husband's Ezer

"It is not good for the man to be alone. I will make a helper as his complement." (Genesis 2:18, HCSB)

A couple of my friends and I started reading the "First 5" daily morning devotional (first5.org) and I love it! As I started this journey through the book of Genesis, God was already speaking to me.

I started reading Genesis 2 about the creation of Adam and Eve. God puts Adam in a deep sleep, takes one rib from his side, closes up the wound, and creates Eve with the rib from Adam. I don't know about you, but I think that's pretty impressive.

I was lying in bed that night after reading this story and a childhood memory popped into my head. I grew up in a very small town with very simple people. Someone had once told me that men actually have one less rib than women. Of course, I believed him at my young age and was amazed with the almighty work of God! In reality, men and women both have the same number of ribs, but that story sparked a desire in me to know God deeper that day. Who knew God would have used that man's story in my future! No, I was not angry at that person for telling me an untrue story about my Heavenly Father. As I remember those words that sweet man told me, I could not help but smile thinking of the excitement in his voice as he told me this story. In that moment, I hoped that he never found out the real truth.

The image of God removing a rib from Adam's side kept playing over and over in my head. God was wanting to tell me something.

I remember Brant had walked through the house with his shoes on my freshly mopped floor. I felt like he did not appreciate the hard work I do to keep our house clean. What really happened was that once he walked across the floor and saw that I had just mopped, he took off his shoes. I felt like it was him against me, and we started arguing. This was a lie from the enemy.

Brant then said something that to this day sticks in my head. He said, "I am on your side." At that moment God was telling me that we are a team; He made us to complement each other.

I could not stop thinking about how God took the rib from Adam and created woman. God was speaking to me. He was trying to tell me, teach me, or show me something I need to hear. So, when I feel Him speak, the first thing I do is open my Bible. I know that is where I will find Him. I went back to Genesis and I read the passage again, and again, and again. I wrote this verse on paper, "Then the Lord God said, 'It is not good for the man to be alone. I will make a helper as his complement" (Genesis 2:18, HCSB).

That word "helper" stood out to me, so I underlined it over and over. Helper. "Father, why this word? What is so important about this word?" I asked.

I pulled out my laptop and searched for the Hebrew word

"helper." I knew I needed to get as close to the original Hebrew word as I could.

The Hebrew translation of helper is *ezer* (pronounced ay'-zer). I had never heard this word before. It was the most beautiful word I had ever seen! I practiced pronouncing it over and over. I wanted to know more about this word.

Dr. Walter Bramson has a blog called "What is an ezer?" It explains that *ezer*, or helper, is used twenty-one times in the Old Testament: twice referring to Eve, three times referred to people helping, and sixteen times in reference to God as a helper against the enemy. These references do not describe this "helper" as someone doing small random acts of kindness, but one of power and importance.

You are probably wondering why this is so important to me and why I'm getting so excited about the word *ezer*.

I never really understood my role as a "wife." I just thought a wife was expected to cook, clean, take care of kids, do laundry, never complain and do what your husband tells you. I was struggling with my role as a wife to Brant because I had lived in the mindset that "I am a slave." My ex-husband would try to use this to control me. During an argument, he would yell, "Submit, woman!" That word always left a bad taste in my mouth. When I hear that word, I cringe. I hated that word. I hated that word because I never truly understood what God intended for that word to mean. I only understood man's misinterpreted, watered down, worldly version. This word was written by God, so this word should bring nothing but joy, love, and excitement.

My sweet, patient, merciful Heavenly Father knew I struggled with this word. He wanted to show me why He created it. He wanted to release me from the devil's misguided use of this word. No longer will I cringe at the sound of this word; this word will from now on only bring me joy. Thank you, Jesus.

Dr. Walter Bramson also said it best when he wrote, "God made Eve to be Adam's protector in a similar fashion as God was Israel's protector… Ezer is a mighty helper and protector of her husband, one who is able to reveal his enemy in times of danger, thus helping to strengthen and protect the marriage."

I am my husband's protector! God has designed all wives to be our husband's *ezer*. I looked at my role as a wife more closely that next morning. I took pride in making sure all the appliances were turned off before we left the house, all the doors were locked, and my husband had clean clothes to wear. Making sure the baby was packed for the day so my husband's morning would run smoothly seemed like such an important task all of a sudden. I wanted to make sure he had a great start to the day, and knowing that I helped make that happen made me honored to have this role. For those wives reading this, pray for ways to be your husbands *ezer* today. Take pride in your role and watch God bless your marriage.

Chapter 17

When God Speaks Through Your Child

After our new daughter was a year old, I was driving down the road and all of a sudden I heard her singing to the song on the radio. I listened intently to this sweet, small voice in the seat behind me, astonished at her ability to memorize the words of this song at her very young age. By this point in her very young life, she was only saying a few words. But out of her mouth I heard, "He knows, He knows," the chorus of a song by Jeremy Camp. Words couldn't express my feelings as my heart overflowed with joy in that moment.

I try to keep a Christian radio station on while in the car with my kids, and after a while I started noticing something different about them. I have seen my children become more aware of God and more excited about getting to know God. I love when I can tell them about a time that God spoke to me through a song when I was having a difficult day. I see this excitement on their faces as they search for songs on their phone to download, hoping to have that same experience. I love hearing my baby girl in the back seat that can only speak a few words sing along to a song as if she is singing praises to God herself!

Then I felt it: the peace of God flowed through me as if He was saying, "Well done, My daughter." Those moments make me search for Him even more. I crave that feeling, the feeling that can only come from my Heavenly Father. I love it when God speaks to me through my children.

I was having a difficult morning that day, feeling rushed and overwhelmed. I dropped the kids off at school, headed to the gym, then to the grocery store. I remember being tired, so tired, and just wanting to go back to bed and sleep for hours, or maybe for days, hoping that I would wake up and the house would be clean, the fridge stocked full of groceries, dinner already cooked, and my family home. No one needed picked up from practice, all the laundry was folded and put away, the baby was bathed, the kids' homework finished and everything ready for the next day. But in the middle of my self-pity, I hear this little voice: "He knows... He knows... Jesus knows."

My little Ava started singing again and I froze in the moment. My heart started to beat fast and my eyes filled with tears. I felt the arms of God wrap around me, and I felt His presence so strong it was as if He was standing right beside me. He knew I was tired. He knew at that moment I felt alone in my suffering. Jesus knows.

I reached down, picked up my daughter, and whispered to her as she wrapped her tiny arms around my neck, "Yes He does, baby girl, He knows."

God reminded me in that moment that He is with me. I found my strength in Him. I felt God calling me a little over a year ago to go part time at work to be home with my family more. With my older two in middle school, I felt this was a critical time for them and I needed to be more available. God called me to cover them in prayer, to be still and listen for Him to tell me when I needed to intercede.

God has shown me so much during this time, mostly how to hand my children over to Him. This was the hardest thing I have ever done as a parent. I watched my daughter struggle through a sport that her father and I felt called to encourage her to try. I sat in the parking lot watching her cry, praying to God for her suffering to stop. I cried myself and questioned if we did the right thing. The devil used that opportunity to struggle with the decision I felt God called me to make.

But God is bigger! He gave her the strength she needed and I started to see His plan unfold. My daughter has grown so much physically, mentally, and spiritually and I firmly believe that God had His hand in every bit of it. What an honor to be able to go to her practice, watch from my car, and cover her in prayer during that time, instead of being at work and feeling disconnected from my kids. I received a blessing from this as well. This gave me hope for how to parent my children. I know God will lead Brant and I as we continue our role as parents.

One day while in the car on the way home from practice, I changed the radio station to country music. My son was in the front seat and he reached up and turned the radio back to the Christian station, looked over at me, and smiled. I smiled back, surprised yet proud of his choice. I thought to myself, "OK, I think I can do this parent thing!" (But only with God's help, of course.)

"Train up a child in the way he should go; even when he is old he will not depart from it." (Proverbs 22:6, HCSB)

"All your children shall be taught by the LORD, and great shall be the peace of your children." (Isaiah 54:13, NKJV)

God has entrusted me with His children while they are here on this earth. I am called to love and nurture them and show them the way to Jesus. They are only with me for a short time and one day they will be with their Heavenly Father for eternity. I'm so grateful that God has blessed me with this privilege as I am so not worthy. And because I am not worthy, I know that I have to rely on Him daily to show me how He wants me to raise His children.

"The person who loves father or mother more than Me is not worthy of Me; the person who loves son or daughter more than Me is not worthy of Me." (Matthew 10:37, HCSB)

I have learned that the more I fill myself with God, the less I feel the need to fill myself with desires of this world.

"God, You are my God; I eagerly seek You. I thirst for You; my body faints for You in a land that is dry, desolate, and without water." (Psalm 63:1, HCSB)

That could be related to relationships, careers or anything that we look to satisfy the void that we all feel at times. The truth is, God is the only one that can truly satisfy our hearts. When I finally figured this out, I found true joy.

"Restore the joy of Your salvation to me, and give me a willing spirit." (Psalm 51:12, HCSB)

True joy has completely transformed my thoughts and actions as a believer. I learned what is truly important in this life. Nothing related to this world satisfied me anymore. Suddenly, I didn't care what my wall colors were, what kind of car I drove, or which neighborhood I lived in. All those things seemed "worldly" to me. I can't take all these things to heaven with me, but I can take people. My focus changed to this sudden, urgent need to tell people about Jesus and live out my life as Christ would want me to. I knew at that moment that I needed to go be Jesus to the world.

"In the same way, let your light shine before men, so that they may see your good works and give glory to your Father in heaven." (Matthew 5:16, HCSB)

Through all my trials, I have become stronger in Christ. Through this relationship, I have found peace and joy. I now know my purpose in this life: to have a personal relationship with the Creator of the world and allow Him to use me according to His will. I know the future for me is uncertain, but I'm so excited to see what He has planned for me. My Father still has a lot to teach me about How to live this life as fully as I can, and with an open heart I will wait for His counsel.

I want to challenge you to completely surrender your life to Him, and He will turn your brokenness into something beautiful. Remember, God uses the broken ones to reveal His glory and power. He will use you if you allow Him. You may be broken and wounded from this life, but I know a healer. His name is Jesus.

Made in the USA
Columbia, SC
05 December 2017